Mira
and Other
Poems of Guyana

Thinking about you,
my Sister, Sylvia.

Zamo

11/13/2020

Mira
and Other
Poems of Guyana

Stanley Niamatali

MOUNTAIN ARBOR
PRESS

Mountain Arbor
Press
Alpharetta, GA

ISBN: 978-1-63183-094-5

Library of Congress Control Number: 2017902090

10 9 8 7 6 5 4 3 2   040317

Printed in the United States of America

⊛This paper meets the requirements of ANSI/NISO Z39.48-1992 (Permanence of Paper)

For My Wife

She rose to His Requirement—dropt
The Playthings of Her Life
To take the honorable Work
Of Woman, and of Wife—

Emily Dickinson

Contents

Acknowledgments

I am grateful to Dr. Racin, Dr. Foster, Dr. Mason, Dr. Jerrolds and Monty, my brother, who believed in me. My special thanks to my colleagues who stood with me through the trials that made this volume possible. I thank Jessica, Aaron and Stephanie for their patience to see the completion of this project. My gratitude also goes to the editors of *The Caribbean Writer* for publishing a version of "The Invite" Vol. 30, 2015.

Introduction

Mira is a narrative poem that details the struggles of a child-bride to matriarch. These interdependent poems blend the essence of the morning with the scent of smoke and spices. The flora and fauna are integral and functional aspects of the narrative as dire cruelty and self-sacrifice are juxtaposed. Dreams are pivotal as they shape and decide the destiny of generations. Mira, like our motherland Guyana that is constantly misused, never loses her capacity to nurture and pare.

Poems of Guyana explore the threshold of the subconscious that cannot be exorcised. Buried images and memories are realized in narratives that are delirious and decorous. They show the dance of beauty and ugliness, kindness and cruelty, innocence and sadness, confusion and conceit in a land where people desecrate the natural gifts of beauty and abuse the freedom within their grasp. Lastly, Our El Dorado reimagines and transforms the legend into an indelible myth.

Prologue (1935)

Mira's Husband

In the top story
of her father's
deeded house,
     Mira's face presses the cool
     redolent floorboards –
     eye peeled to the crack.
Below,
     naked walls frame
     the bed of torment
     with her landlord-husband
     and the hapless widow –
her calves on meaty shoulders
and unseemly soles treading air
like a dying duck –
     who gapes with sadness
     at Mira's quiet eye.

1966

Smash e[1] Head

In the kitchen
    a lone dim bulb
    hangs from a cord
    with sleeping flies
    as thick and close
    as a panicle of paddy.
Mira
puts the karahee[2]
over the greenheart fire,
picks up the smooth lohar,[3]
cracks the peppercorns,
pounds tumeric root,
smashes garlic cloves
and grinds them
on her dead mother's masala brick.
Adding just enough water,
she blends them with curry
powder and garam masala
into a smooth paste
that she stirs with the long handle
enameled spoon into hot oil
that bubbles and sizzles
Sunday morning curry.

---

[1] his
[2] Bowl-shaped frying pan; wok
[3] semi-round pestle used for grinding

Bu'n[4] e Rass[5]

Stirring the swamp
of water, flour, salt
and baking powder,
the mix leeches
onto her hand
like years of weighted
memories.
She squeezes and rubs
the stickiness from her fingers
and presses with her palm
until there is agreement
and the coming together
in a single ball of dough.
The loose floorboards
by the fireside
creak as she stirs
the cut-up chicken
into the karahee.
The fowlcock[6] crows
as she taps the spoon
on the karahee's rim,
covers it and pulls
at the firewood
for a slow fire.

---

[4] burn
[5] vulgar: asshole
[6] rooster

Poison e Rass

Compliant dough
spreads dutifully
under the pressure
of the rolling pin
clicking under
Mira's wedding band.

With nimble fingertips,
she pinches and palms
the circle of dough
and plasters it
onto the hot
cast-iron taawaa[7].

Fragrance of baking roti
pervades the subtle smoke
of the tempering fire.

Awakened,
rising like a breathing lung,
this perfect crossover
is clapped, folded, placed
in the white basin
and covered
with the white roti-cloth.

---

[7] griddle without a handle

The Dog in Meh[8] House

The wind,
        cool off the Berbice River,
enters
        through the half-open
        kitchen door
with the green fragrance
        of a lilac morning
awaiting
        that resplendent sunrise.

Mira's children
wipe curried chicken
        from their flowered enameled plates
        with pieces of soft roti.

Climbing the kitchen steps,
her husband,
        unremorseful as a bad fire,
comes from his sleep-out[9].

Stink
        from the fissure
        he was caulking
arouses flies
        that light on food, cup rims,
        plates, fingers and faces.

---

[8] my
[9] whoring; philandering

His fingers,
        reeking of fetid flesh,
poke roti
        into his chewing mouth.

Mira,
        unwraps the white roti-cloth,
gives him the last piece
        and shakes the crumbs
        for the yard fowl
        under her window.

Meh Guh[10] Kill e

Mira,
  alone,
dabs margarine
  on the unwanted
  piece of broken bread
and lets it melt
  on the still-warm
  taawaa.
She runs water
  into the empty karahee
and piles dirty plates
  into the sink.

Table wiped clean,
the flies migrate
  to the hanging cord.
She tilts the teapot
as the leaf-dregs dance
and swirl in her cup.

---

[10] will

But How?

Sitting on the kitchen steps,
Mira soaks her fried bread
    in the tepid tea,
and looks at her maiden-hair ferns
verdurous under the guava tree.

How they grow –
    she remembers the brown furry root
    she nestled in a handful of dirt
    and swaddled in damp coconut husk.

The Dominique hen
lifts its head from the dirt
and looks at Mira.

The calico,
    balanced on the picket fence,
waves at a passing monarch.

The blue sakis[11],
    full of angst,
shriek and dance
    among ripe guavas.

The three note
Kiskadee
    repeats its refrain:
Kiskadee! Kiskadee!

---

[11] blue tangers

1935

Talking to Her Husband

Distressed with a crusted pot,
Mira is at the sink;
her tears mixing with suds.

Fifteen year old bride,
tormented by a crack,
stares at the floorboards
as she sets the tea
before him and mumbles:

    "Meh can see."

Still chewing,
he grabs hair,
stands upright,
works the face,
flings the annoyance
across the kitchen,
sits and slurps
his sweet tea.

Light Side of Sleep

Flying across the road,
the monarch lights
on the red zinnia
next to her father,
who stands tall.
He smiles and tilts
the fresh green bamboo basket
laden with the joyous fruits
of her childhood:
bananas, mangoes,
cidums, star apples,
ginnip, tangerines,
sappodillas ,
cherries and plums.
Beside him,
her mother,
smiling, cradles
a long papaya
across her breast
and extends a leathery-
skin mami in her right hand.
Mira closes her eyes
against forlorn tears.

Dark Side of Sleep

Mira opens her eyes
to a brown
sunless afternoon sky
raining the spiral ash
of burned sugar-cane leaves.
Across the road,
a desiccated bee persists
with the parched zinnia.
Mira's father
tilts the bamboo basket
of babies' bloody heads.
Mira's mother,
holds an infant
to her breast,
and offers Mira
its severed head.

Deliver Me

Through the thin mattress
stuffed with coconut
fiber, the bed springs
stencil Mira's back
with her husband's hammering.
Face to the wall,
she closes her eyes.

Running Away

Mira unknots her homemade
handkerchief, takes a florin
for the Berbice
River crossing
and Georgetown train.

Sitting on the slatted
wooden seat, she feels
the wind's rush
sweet on her face
as banana leaves
buddy-slap
the swaying carriages.

At Maichony, she leans
through the window, smells
the hot pepper sauce, fried
banga mary, fresh bread,
polourie, sweets and fruits.
She buys pointer sweety,[12]
nutten[13] and is happy
wondering what to say
to her brother she never met.

---

[12] hard candy on a stick
[13] sweet peanut butter biscuit similar to Italian Amaretti cookie

Sin of the Father

Standing in his white
Victorian doorway,
his white head
moves from her tiny feet
to her just-powdered face.

You are not my sister!

He closes
his heavy Victorian door.

Waiting in the Rain

Mira,
       sheltering under the portico
       of Kwall's General Goods,
stares at the pelting rain
as it bounces off the pavement
and soaks her shoes.

No Choice

Late,
Mira runs through
the incessant rain
and thunder to the station
on Carmichael Street
for the last seat
at the broken window,
hopeless against the rain.

Crossing back
to New Amsterdam,
shoes in hand,
cold from the rain
and hot with fever,
Mira walks homeward
to her husband, lotus-seated
like a buddha, grossly
unlike the Buddha.

Her frock, wet as a floor-cloth[14],
falls from her slender shoulders.
She bows, prostrates and kisses
his nakedness.

---

[14] rag used for washing floors

Another Choice

Mira turns
from her ash-free fireside,
damp and shiny
with daubed cow dung and mud.
Everything washed and dried,
in its place.
       Pepper in its corner.
       Pot-spoon on its nail.
       Sun-bleached roti towel,
       neatly folded.
       Flies rest on the cord
       with the fading thyme.
She thinks of sleep
and that happy draught
of fate.

Elixir

Will it be bitter?
Will it be sweet?
Should she drink it with tea?
Should she drink it with milk
and leave her bare cup, unfulfilled?

Goodbye

Mira descends the stairs
for the slim amber bottle
with the smiling skull
that's nestled among
her maiden-hair ferns
under the shade
of the guava tree.

She wants to see them,
one
last
time,
to feel their fine leaves
caress
her caring fingers
one
last
time.

Mater

Mira sees the little worms
stretched on her ferns'
wiry spines.
Looking into
the painted pot,
she sees hopeful shoots
peeping from the rich
black soil.

She uncorks
the amber bottle
and pours the clear poison
with a pint of water into
the flit can and begins
spritzing her ferns.
Finished, she climbs
the stairs for the flies.

1968

Funeral

The organ grieves.
The casket plods as slowly
as a lumbering locust –
pauses on mahogany
legs for a final view.

Mira,
       in the second pew,
looks at the casket –
an open album.
Her brother, asleep
like her dead father.

Perfume of roses
and wormwood
floats past her
dark lace veil
along with a voice
as clean and clear
as that blind
Phoenician's.

> *How 'e[15] did want*
> *to see e[16] sister*
> *in New Amsterdam.*
> *Always. Always*

---

[15] he
[16] his

talkin' 'bout
she big business,
she doctor sons.

The Fish

At the sloping mud-flat
of the Berbice River,
Mira's husband
stands on the dry log.
He sees the muddy fish
slapping its tail
and sends the flat-man[17],
Mr. Singh, to get it.
Washed clean,
the four foot
live snapper
glories in its red,
orange and yellow.
Neighbors on their bridges
gawk as he parades
his gift up the strand.

---

[17] places turnbuckle and wire rope around logs to be winched from
the mudflat

The Stupid Rass

Mira,
       seeing her husband
       lay the great fish
       on the heavy plank table
       under the mango tree,
pleads:

       Le' meh clean am[18].
       Yuh never clean fish.

He rakes the cutlass
across its back,
scales flying.

Eviscerated,
the open-eyed snapper
stares from the plank.

       Ow,
       nuh[19] chop am.
       Cut am with wan knife
       so yuh nuh mash am.

The cutlass, raised above his head,
descends, and the fish flops,
its tough skin

---

[18] it
[19] don't

34

holding its mangled
flesh and bones.

In a carnal frenzy,
he whacks and whacks.
Flesh, skin and bones
fly through the air.
Yard fowl are busy,
and two Muscovies
nod to each other
as they tug on some skin.
The calico,
in the ginnip tree,
tilts its head to chew.

He drops the cutlass
and leaves.
Mira's tears fall
into the bowl of abused flesh.

Buy' a Cow in the Bush

With the two o'clock sun
hot on his neck, he leaves
Mira and their youngest
with his Morris Minor
and walks up the back dam
to find his yet-to-see bull.

As the sun turns yellow
behind the possessed silk cotton,
he returns empty handed
as the day he paid
for the brindled-bull
everybody see
among the bizzee-bizzee[20].

Mira,
not looking at him,
says she will be back
and slips into the privacy
of the tall bizzee-bizzee.

His horn blaring,
Mira returns,
her pleated dress
cradles the green
pods of cribbage cole.

---

[20] tall grass

At home,
her children
are excited to eat,
for the first time,
wild cribbage cole,
saltfish and hot rice.

1970

Look at Him Now

While the maid pokes
his soiled linens
with a broomstick
in the white basin
of water and Jarvex[21],
Mira,
her finger poking the washcloth,
rubs clean his gums,
palette and tongue.
His body washed;
his soft mottled back
unctioned and powdered.
Mira slips his arms,
        hanger-thin with their flaccid skin,
through the qurta[22] sleeves
and pulls it over his shoulders,
        remembering her babies
        in oversized chemise.

---

[21] bleach; chlorine
[22] large oversized shirt; Muslim shirt that is as big as a nightshirt

Finally

In the dawn
on a weekday,
alone,
Mira labors
for her children's
unexpected
treat.

As they gather
at the table
for their chanced feast,
Mira,
alone,
without a maid,
attends her husband.

Mira's children pull at the roti,
daubing curry.

> *Bai[23], Come!*
> *Yuh[24] dadee[25].*
> *'e dead!*

He is on his side.
His last dribble,

---

[23] boy
[24] your
[25] father

yellow bile,
blots the fresh
pillow case.

Smoke

Go 'way!
Smoke hay[26]*!*
Go 'way,
so smoke nuh get in yuh eye'.

Mira's youngest sees
       linens,
              heavy with vomit,
              kerosene and smoke
          hanging from the iron rod,
just before they balloon
into a ball of fire.

---

[26] here

Forever Amber

Clinging to the yellow brick
    like the pounded sugar crystals
    from the too big-for-his-mouth
    bullseye sweetie,
he sees the crushed glass.

At his feet,
    among the cracks
    in the concrete,
amber flakes
sparkle in sunlight.

Epilogue (1975)

Between the
Road and the River

Under the sheltering trees,
the calico is asleep
on the cool iron bench
beside the potted ferns.

Flassie, curled
on the fresh softwood
shavings, is snoring.

The colorful crossbreed fowl
dust their feathers and lay flat
their wings for the filtered light.

Mira,
in her hammock
anchored to the mango
and guava trees,
gently sways –
here and there,
then and now,
kip and kindle.

He Speaks

Meh been a think.
Meh been hay sick
for mo' than wan year.

Mira
       looks
       at the strange
       man talking.

Meh sarry[27].
Meh sarry
how meh beat yuh,
how meh treat yuh.
Ow. Meh sarry.

Tears fall from his face
onto Mira's arm.

Meh nuh want
live like this.
Help meh.
Meh beg yuh.
Help meh.
Gimme something.
Meh beg yuh.

---

[27] sorry

Peace Porridge

Stirring the gray
plantain pap,
Mira adds
Carnation milk,
course brown sugar crystals,
a shred of cinnamon
and that clear liquid.
Instinctively,
her quick finger
and quick lick
test for sweetness.

R.I.P.

Mira feels
his soft lips,
closed,
on her mouth.
Confusion
runs from her scalp,
down her neck and into her spine.

Mingled breath.
      Her first kiss.
Their first kiss,
      their last.

Other
Guyana Poems

Decoction

Night Journey – The Grip

The last bite of brokmouth
     lay on the stelling floor
before that sleeping dog,
     its tired skin, scarred
     and broken from years
     of sores, mange, fleas and men.

I step onto the gangplank.

The bell's clear and simple clang.

The purring wire rope
     winches the heavy ramp.
Gears ring into place.

The revved engine murmurs
     along the metal deck,
     my legs, spine and into my hand
     at ease on the empty capstan.

New Amsterdam says goodbye,
and the Rosignol beacon
     comes to me on a dark breeze.

Slipping on the same wet grass,
my suitcase,
     laden with hot
     pepper, photographs of people
     and places, substance of years,

black LP records, layer
upon layer, invisible
          cloak of ghosts, shirts of sunshine
          and spite, a serpentine belt,
          mirror of secret kisses,
double-edged razor blade, stains,
sachet of knotted memories,
          a naked tamarind seed,
          touch of intimates, musk, cut
          and uncut, a brush of tangled
hair, mud from kneeling
          at the river, tapes
          tightly wound, a Rubik's cube
          of schoolboy's dreams
and a broken clock,
          pulls me to the cold deep
          of this black black river.

My fingers will not unfurl
to release my heavy grip.

Insane

Radica Singh,
      tormented by the music
      from that Geiger place,
dances and holds villagers –
      believers of ole higue,
      flying ball of fire,
      shapeshifter that sucks
      the blood of babies –
with her unblinking eyes.

Along the sandy roadside,
      on the dark pillow of her blood,
she rests her bludgeoned head.

Birdman

Early morning.

>   Cruising down the strand
>   on his new Raleigh,
> proud banner,
>   flagpole rigid,
> holds the cage
>   of his twattiling twatwa[28].

> Young men,
>   framed and duplicated
>   in windows,
> eye his brazen songbird.

Late afternoon.

>   Cruising down the strand
>   with his new wife
>   in his new Toyota,
> Birdman nods to the "Material Girl"
>   floating through his window
> with his smoke
> from his State Express.

> Men,
>   hand in pocket,
> suck sugarcane

---

[28] songbird

and eye
>his bobbing copper-colored wife
>in her black tank top.

Night.

>Leaving for business in the US,
>Birdman walks past his mingling dogs,
>backs out in his SUV,
>stops,
>looks up at his verandah,
>counts his hanging cages,
>lights his State Express
>and leaves his wife
>standing alone
>>behind his louvers
>>and his ironwork.

Day Clean.

>>Folded over Birdman's verandah,
>his brother,
>>shirtless,
>hawks slime from his sleep.
>>Beside him,
>the white-faced parrot,
>>screaming,
>flaps its wings,
>showing off its hidden
>scarlet feathers.

The Invite

Brylcreemed and cooled
with Old Spice,
Paul,
       logging worker,
crosses the bridge,
and looks at the guppies
schooled in the shadows
of the blooming
bleeding hearts.

Clothes crispy new,
Paul,
smiling,
exits the minibus in La Penitence.
       Her cut-eye;
       her veiled smile.
He smiles.
The trees,
       in their slow
       sway across the road,
shelter him with tenderness.

In the office,
Paul,
       fresh from his six month stint
       in the bush, awaits his pay.
His furtive eye,
       wishing

for her July smile,
    her Christmas smile,
blind to the snickers.

Confirming the address
on the gilt-edged wedding
invitation, he stands
before the black gates
of the funeral home.

Dressed for love --
        the Carefesta[29] monkey.
The braying jackass.
Invitation,
now,
        as heavy as flypaper.
Heat rising like a fever.
Myopia of truth.
Distilled sweetness of love,
a bitter-cup of shame.

Open koker[30] – effluvium.
Slow dance of a floating
carcass. Sick-eyed dog,
host to a healthy
legion of mange.
Dreams of her Diana
dish writhing with maggots.

---

[29] Celebration similar to a carnival
[30] Sluice – gate to regulate drainage and irrigation

Above, dark cumulus.
The filarial vendor,
        her inflated Popeye legs
        too heavy for walking,
opens her umbrella
before her ripe mangoes.
Paul, on one knee,
takes the sealed envelope
        from his pocket,
places it in her hand
and walks off in the rain.

A Bucket of Water

Ribboned braids
resting on white blouse.
Pleated skirt.
White socks pulled
to her camphored shins.

First Monday for school--
          new shoes, rainbow pencils
          and sky-blue exercise books --
pipe dry.

Friends, flutie[31], poulourie[32]
and sour[33] on her mind,
plastic bucket swinging
with her fresh morning gait.
Rain-soaked grass and vines
lick at her ankles.

She reaches the muddy foot-path
that slopes to the trench. She stops.
The vrooming hummingbird
pauses before her.
Her grass-seeded feet
step onto the wet track.
She skids down the mud-slick bank
into the basin of light.

---

[31] iced-cube size popcicle
[32] similar to falafel
[33] condiment made with lime juice, hot peppers and spices

Unrefined

The Miser and the Flirt

Seeing him Judge-serious,
     his sourie-sized[34] fingers
     touching his checkered
     shirt pocket
     where he keeps
     my promised check,
I laugh
remembering the beautiful
secretary giving me
the printed receipt.

Judge-serious,
I look into her brown eyes.

     This was just a piece
     of paper until
     it was touched
     by the most beautiful
     of hands. Now
     I will fold it
     and put it
     in my shirt pocket
     where it will be
     the closest thing
     to the deepest
     chambers of my heart.

---

[34] highly acidic green fruit

Showing strong unbraced white teeth,
she said I was full of it.
Then we had tea.

Microwave or Fireside

Them young gal[35],
them a' like
microwave.
Ding. Heat up.
Quick time. Done.
Can't cook nothing.

Me,
      with me hard
      old cowheel,
want wan[36] heavy pot
and wan slow fire.

---

[35] young woman
[36] a; one

The Politics of Monkey Jack
(Reported in *The Guyana Chronicle*)

Across the Berbice River,
in the town of New Amsterdam
      where the dead
      outnumber
      the living
      and derelict houses
      with broken and missing
      windows face each other
      in their quiet emptiness,
Jack rides his dog,
      Clifford,
around crater-
      sized potholes
into the yard
      of the once august house.

There he dismounts, climbs
bare-assed the weathered
and brittle steps, jumps
on the window-sill
and disappears.

Eileen,
      eyes bulging,
says:

Jack open'
she house window,

lift up she blind,
take off she pot cover,
throw 'way she pot cover,
put 'e hand in she pot,
stir it up
drink she milk
an' nuh lef'
one drap[37] for
she pickney[38].

After suffering
       years of Jack's wotlessness[39],
Mr. Wilburg, scantling lean,
       says that thieving Jack
       will not leave.
       Jack got it fat.
The community went looking
       for Jack, but Jack retreated
       to his Cooper Lane's residence.
At this shaky house,
       their Jamarat[40],
residence unloaded their weight
of broken bricks, bottles and stones.

They say Jack run
       to #2 village
where he resides
       without portfolio.

---

[37] drop
[38] children
[39] wickedness
[40] Jamarat is one of three pillars that represents the devil that is stoned
during the Hajj ritual

73

Youth Rally –
The Minister's Speech

We only just broke the shackles
of imperialism and must
now dissociate ourselves ....

turning from the wet grass
brilliant in the sun,
he sees soft amber
hanging from her ear --
slow jalebi[41] syrup

Taste the sweetness of freedom....

that mouth, oh, opulent plum

I say Carpe Diem ....

ponder that handful
of mahanboug[42];
oh, gentle doily peel;
lips knead sweet dough;
tongue that rude raisin.

---

[41] small funnel-cake
[42] sweetmeat with raisin; consistency of soft fudge

Yes, Guyana's young....

    stomach, firm smoothness
of freshly peeled cassava.

Explore that new horizon ....

    finger, slipping between
warm sour-sweet-doubles[43],
beyond that veined channa[44].

Embrace your destiny....

easy give of gulab jamun.

Be one with your dreams....

    badam lacha!

---

[43] Sandwich of two pita-like falafel made from split-pea flour
[44] Chikpea; garbanzo beans

From the Jungle

Our Greenheart

Guyana's forest.
Tedium. Duplication.
Homogeny of bush, shrubs and trees.
Suddenly,
this still point.
This solitaire,
the most singular of trees.
Fibonaccied.
Oh great greenheart --
our cathedral,
our temple,
our minaret,
our heritage,
rising, rising, rising ....

And how shall we, dispossessed,
presume when back-step
officials' self-serving hands
still reek of the putrid meat
from overlords' backwash?

Native Son

Akeem Hyles[45].
Son. Brother.
Martyred defending
our Guyana
from her sons, wotless[46].

And many
will have withered,
but you will remain
that lone cruda[47]
facing the tide –
forever green.

---

[45] Guyana Police constable drowned while on patrol to halt illegal mining
[46] wicked; worthless; wanton
[47] mangrove tree

Our Eldorado

From the soupy grave
of warm palm oil
and sallow mud,
    eyes closed,
Eldorado rises and,
    from head to toe,
is dusted with finest gold.

From the dank cave,
    between night and day,
Eldorado comes forth,
    the walking relic.

Below, the open-mouthed
black lake sobs softly
onto the silent sand.
The wind blows,
and a somber rain falls
on the swooning trees.
The oblique insipid light
shows solemn shadows.
Hot tears overflow
their tender eyes,
warm their faces
and melt into the sand.
Through agonizing eyes,
they behold their dear
sweet son, a wisp
before the cave of nothingness.

From the black rock,
        quick as a meteor,
Eldorado,
        a burnished flash,
sizzles into the abyss –
        the ripples of a deep kiss.

Undulating lilies
waft their essence
to the rafts where men
dutifully paddle
to the concentric
watery rose. There,
        in its whorled center,
they cast the anathema --
uncorrupted gold --
into the vaulted
and alluring depths.

The rain stops;
earnest supplicants
break chains,
unfinger rings,
unlock bracelets,
all gold,
and cast them
into the gulping
watery lips.

The resolute lake,
        showing nothing of its depth,
lithographs the boundless sky.
A voluptuous swell

rolls across its face
to the shore. A great big
     and beautiful silverfish,
     streaked with gold, rises.
Her iris,
     a wheel of golden spokes
     sprocketed by a black pearl.
Water flows over her back,
     mirroring the suddenly golden sun.
The devout prostrate
on the rafts and sand
     as she disappears to her
     Elysium depth.
Opening their dutiful eyes,
they behold Eldorado
afloat on the lake.

Eldorado,
     his nakedness,
     covered with a rough cloth,
lies on slippery
green banana leaves.
His mother,
     kneeling,
breathes into his mouth.
Sacred water gushes
     from his lips as he opens
his brown eyes flecked
     with gold.

Glowworms
punctuate leaves.
The petal-strewn anaconda

asleep in its hide.
Bugs embrace twigs.
A frog squats on a succulent spine.
Marmosets genuflect in trees
where orchid blooms waver.
Orioles, busy with banana.
Corn with silken flax
roast over ruby coals.
Plantain chips bubble
in palm oil.
Calabash of palm wine.
Pineapple mandalas.
A jaguar dozes
on a lazy limb.
Sunlight pierces the water
with its staff.
All. All, auriferous.

And above this land
        that is El Dorado,
the harpy eagle,
        its wings spread
        across the sky,
circles this lost world,
        its forlorn cry a fading wrinkle
        in our twilight paradise.

About the Author

Stanley Niamatali is a Professor of English at Montgomery College, Maryland. *Oberon, Full Circle, Anthology of Appalachian Writers* and *The Caribbean Writer* have published his poetry. His first book, *The Hinterlands*, published by the Caribbean Press won The Guyana Prize for First Book of Poetry in 2015.

Other Books by Author

The Hinterlands